The Pledge of Allegiance

Introducing Primary Sources

by Kathryn Clay

CAPSTONE PRESS
a capstone imprint

Little Explorer is published by Capstone Press,
1710 Roe Crest Drive, North Mankato, Minnesota 56003
www.mycapstone.com

The name of the Smithsonian Institution and the sunburst logo are registered trademarks of
the Smithsonian Institution. For more information, please visit www.si.edu.

Library of Congress Cataloging-in-Publication Data
Cataloging-in-publication information is on file with the Library of Congress.
ISBN 978-1-4914-8227-8 (library binding)
ISBN 978-1-4914-8611-5 (paperback)
ISBN 978-1-4914-8617-7 (eBook PDF)

Editorial Credits
Michelle Hasselius, editor; Richard Parker, designer; Wanda Winch, media researcher;
Steve Walker, production specialist

Our very special thanks to Jennifer L. Jones, Chair, Armed Forces Division at the National Museum
of American History, Kenneth E. Behring Center, Smithsonian, for her curatorial review. Capstone
would also like to thank Kealy Gordon, Product Development Manager, and the following at
Smithsonian Enterprises: Ellen Nanney, Licensing Manager; Brigid Ferraro, Vice President, Education
and Consumer Products; Carol LeBlanc, Senior Vice President, Education and Consumer Products.

Photo Credits
Capstone, 15 (bottom); Collection of the Supreme Court of the United States, 29; Department of
Rare Books and Special Collections, Rush Rhees Library, University of Rochester, 6 (right), 15 (top);
Dreamstime: Americanspirit, 25, Piet Hagenaars, 9; Franklin D. Roosevelt Library, 20; iStockphoto:
Jani Bryson, cover; Library of Congress: Prints and Photographs Division, 6 (left), 7, 10, 12, 13 (all), 16,
17, 22; Shutterstock: Andrea Izzotti, 21, Arevik, paper design, Dan Thornberg, 8, Joseph Sohm, 24, M
Dogan, 18; Thinkstock: Big Cheese Photo, 11; U.S. Air National Guard: TSgt Joseph Harwood, 19; West
Virginia State Archives, 23; www.plaquesandletters.com, 5; Youth's Companion (09-08-1892), Box 9,
Folder 5, Youth's Companion, MS1998.002, Cleveland Colby Colgate Archives, Colby-Sawyer College,
4, 28

Printed in the United States of America in North Mankato, Minnesota.
009221CGS16

Table of Contents

Primary Sources

What is a primary source? A primary source is a piece of evidence. It gives proof of a time or place in history. People use primary sources to answer questions about the past.

446   THE YOUTH'S COMPANION.   SEPTEMBER 8, 1892.

National School Celebration of Columbus Day.

THE OFFICIAL PROGRAMME.

Let every pupil and friend of the Schools who reads THE COMPANION, at once present personally the following programme to the Teachers, Superintendents, School Boards, and Newspapers in the towns and cities in which they reside. Not one School in America should be left out in this Celebration.

446   THE YOUTH'S COMPANION.   SEPTEMBER 8, 1892.

National School Celebration of Columbus Day.

THE OFFICIAL PROGRAMME.

Let every pupil and friend of the Schools who reads THE COMPANION, at once present personally the following programme to the Teachers, Superintendents, School Boards, and Newspapers in the towns and cities in which they reside. Not one School in America should be left out in this Celebration.

In obedience to an Act of Congress, the President on July 21 issued a Proclamation recommending that October 21, the 400th Anniversary of the Discovery of America, be celebrated everywhere in America by suitable exercises in the schools.

A uniform Programme for every school in America, to be used on Columbus Day, simultaneously with the dedicatory exercises of the World's Columbian Exposition grounds in Chicago, will give an impressive unity to the popular celebration. Accordingly, when the Superintendents of Education, last February, accepted THE COMPANION'S plan for this national Public School celebration, they instructed their Executive Committee to prepare an Official Programme of exercises for the Day, uniform for every school. To enable preparations for the National School Celebration to begin *immediately*, this Executive Committee now publish through THE COMPANION

THE OFFICIAL PROGRAMME

for the National Columbian Public School Celebration

It has been a pleasure to THE COMPANION to contribute, as its special gift, the Original Poems and the Address which are to be rendered on the occasion.

Contributed by The Youth's Companion.

THE ODE FOR COLUMBUS DAY.

"COLUMBIA'S BANNER."

"God helping me," cried Columbus, "though fair or foul the breeze,
I will sail and sail till I find the land beyond the western seas!"—
So an eagle might leave its eyrie, bent, though the blue should bar,
To fold its wings on the loftiest peak of an undiscovered star!
And into the vast and void abyss he followed the setting sun;
Nor gulfs nor gales could fright his sails till the wondrous quest was done.
But O the weary vigils, the murmuring, torturing days,
Till the Pinta's gun, and the shout of "Land!" set the black night ablaze!

lay ready for a new experiment in civilization. All things were ready. New forces had come to light, full of overturning power in the Old World. In the New World they were to work together with a mighty harmony.

It was for Columbus, propelled by this fresh life, to reveal the land where these new forces were to be given space for development, and where the awaited trial of the new civilization was to be made. To-day we reach our most memorable milestone. We look backward and we look forward.

Backward, we see the first mustering of modern ideas; their long conflict with Old World theories, which were also transported hither. We see stalwart men and brave women, one moment on the shore, disappearing in dim forests. We hear the axe. We see the flame of burning cabins and hear the cry of the savage. We see the never-ceasing wagon trains always toiling westward. We behold log cabins becoming villages, then cities. We watch the growth of institutions out of little beginnings—schools becoming an educational system;

the pledge was printed in *The Youth's Companion* in 1892

Primary sources might be photos, letters, or drawings. The Pledge of Allegiance is also a primary source.

Pledge of Allegiance at a Glance

- written by Francis Bellamy
- written in 1892
- first printed in *The Youth's Companion* magazine on September 8, 1892
- two changes have been made to pledge
- currently has 31 words

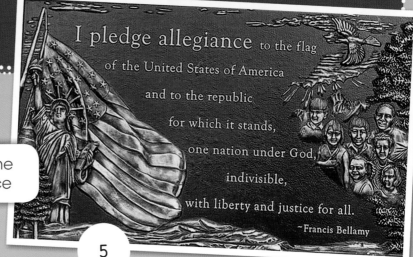

bronze plaque of the Pledge of Allegiance

I pledge allegiance to the flag of the United States of America and to the republic for which it stands, one nation under God, indivisible, with liberty and justice for all.

~Francis Bellamy

Writing the Pledge

Francis Bellamy wrote the Pledge of Allegiance in 1892 to celebrate Columbus Day. Bellamy was an editor for the magazine, *The Youth's Companion.* On September 8, 1892, the magazine printed Bellamy's pledge.

portrait of Francis Bellamy

This painting from 1893 shows Columbus arriving in San Salvador.

FACT

Christopher Columbus sailed to America in 1492. Four hundred years later, more than 12 million children across the country said the Pledge of Allegiance to honor this event.

Thousands of children read *The Youth's Companion* each week. Bellamy hoped students would see the pledge and say it at school. He sent hundreds of copies to schools all over the country.

The Youth's Companion

Nathaniel Willis started *The Youth's Companion* in Boston, Massachusetts, in 1827. Sixty years later almost half a million people were reading the magazine. It printed the works of famous writers, including Emily Dickinson and Mark Twain.

portrait of Nathaniel Willis in 1923

A Symbol of Respect and Loyalty

A pledge is a promise. Pledging allegiance means you promise to be loyal. Saying the Pledge of Allegiance shows loyalty and respect for the U.S. flag and our country.

FACT

The U.S. flag is a symbol of freedom. The 13 stripes stand for the original 13 colonies. The 50 stars stand for the 50 states.

Pledge of Allegiance statues at the Brookgreen Gardens in Pawleys Island, South Carolina

A Morning Tradition

Teachers and students liked saying the Pledge of Allegiance. Soon many classrooms were saying it each morning. Students said the pledge before they started their lessons.

In this 1899 photo, children say the Pledge of Allegiance at school.

In 1898 New York passed a law requiring students to say the pledge every day in school. Other states passed similar laws. By 2012 there were only five states without laws about the pledge.

In this 1943 photo, children salute the flag during the Pledge of Allegiance.

Today people say the pledge with their hands over their hearts. But when it was first written, people used the Bellamy salute. The Bellamy salute looks like a military salute. People placed their right hands on their foreheads. They pointed a hand toward the U.S. flag when they said, "To the flag for which it stands."

FACT

During World War II (1939–1945), people stopped using the Bellamy salute. It looked too similar to the German Nazi salute.

Nazi soldiers salute Adolf Hitler in 1939

students in Connecticut use the Bellamy salute in 1942

Changing the Pledge

The Pledge of Allegiance has changed two times since 1892. At first it had only 23 words. In 1923 "my flag" was changed to "the flag of the United States." A year later it was changed to "the flag of the United States of America."

I pledge allegiance
to my flag
and to the Republic
for which it stands,
one Nation indivisible,
with liberty and
justice for all.
—original Pledge of Allegiance, 1892

A pledge of allegiance suggested for the Columbus Day salute to the Flag – F.B.

I pledge allegiance to my Flag and to the Republic for which it stands – One Nation indivisible – with liberty and justice for all

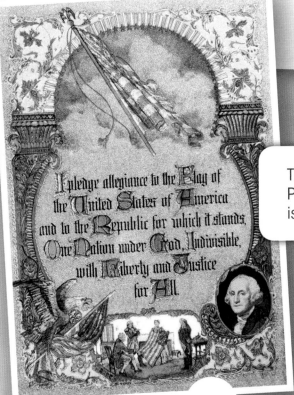

I pledge allegiance to the Flag of the United States of America and to the Republic for which it stands, One Nation under God, Indivisible, with Liberty and Justice for All.

This version of the Pledge of Allegiance is used today.

In 1954 President Dwight D. Eisenhower wanted to change the pledge again. He added "under God."

portrait of President Dwight D. Eisenhower

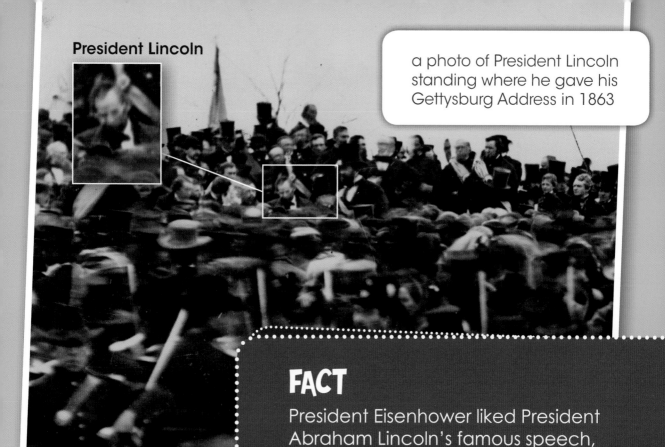

President Lincoln

a photo of President Lincoln standing where he gave his Gettysburg Address in 1863

FACT

President Eisenhower liked President Abraham Lincoln's famous speech, the Gettysburg Address. Lincoln used the words "under God" when he gave his address in 1863.

Some people did not like this change, including Bellamy's daughter. She wanted to keep the pledge the way it was. Congress voted to add the new words on June 14, 1954. This version of the Pledge of Allegiance is still used today.

The Flag Code

At first there were no rules about how to say the Pledge of Allegiance. Then on June 14, 1923, the National Flag Conference met in Washington, D.C. They created the Flag Code. The Flag Code explained how to say the Pledge of Allegiance. It also described how to properly handle and display the U.S. flag.

post office building in Washington, D.C.

A member of a U.S. Air Force Honor Guard teaches students in Ohio how to properly fold the flag.

FACT

Flag Day became a national holiday in 1949. It is celebrated each year on June 14.

In 1942 President Franklin D. Roosevelt made the Flag Code part of U.S. law. This meant the government could make changes to the pledge.

President Franklin D. Roosevelt in 1941

capitol building in Washington, D.C.

Although it is part of U.S. law, people cannot be punished for breaking the Flag Code. But U.S. citizens are expected to treat the flag and the pledge with respect.

A Day in Court

Many children liked saying the Pledge of Allegiance at school. But others did not. They took their case to court in 1943. The U.S. Supreme Court said children could not be forced to say the pledge at school.

photo of the U.S. Supreme Court justices in 1941

More than 70 years later, people still argue about the pledge. In 2004 the U.S. Supreme Court ruled to keep "under God" in the pledge.

West Virginia Board of Education versus Barnette

Members of the Jehovah's Witnesses religion did not want to be forced to say the Pledge of Allegiance in school. They argued that saying the pledge was against their religion. The U.S. Supreme Court agreed. The court ruled children could not be forced to say the pledge. Doing so would take away their right to free speech.

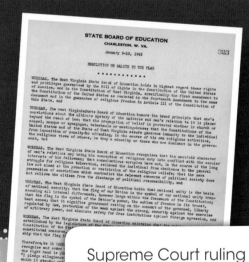

Supreme Court ruling in *West Virginia Board of Education versus Barnette*

Who Still Says the Pledge?

The pledge can still be heard in schools across the country. But children are not the only people who say it. People say the pledge when they become U.S. citizens. Members of Congress have said the pledge before meetings since 1999. Boy Scouts and Girl Scouts say the pledge at their events. City officials sometimes say the pledge before city meetings.

pamphlet from the U.S. Department of Justice welcoming new U.S. citizens

U.S. Department of Justice
Immigration and Naturalization Service

A Welcome to U.S.A. Citizenship

Pledge of Allegiance to the Flag

*

I pledge allegiance to the flag of the United States of America and to the Republic for which it stands, one Nation *under God*, indivisible, with liberty and justice for all.

> *"The national Pledge of Allegiance is one of America's most treasured national symbols, and it serves an invaluable unifying purpose."*
> —2013 Congressional Prayer Caucus

In this photo from 2005, a Boy Scout troop says the Pledge of Allegiance.

Meaning of the Pledge

"I pledge allegiance to the flag of the United States of America."

meaning: I promise to be loyal to our country, the United States of America.

"And to the Republic for which it stands"

meaning: A republic is a free country. The flag stands for our country.

"One nation, under God, indivisible,"

meaning: All the states make up one country and cannot be divided.

"With liberty and justice for all."

meaning: All U.S. citizens receive the same freedoms and rights.

Timeline

At a signal from the Principal the pupils, in ordered ranks,
hands to the side, face the Flag. Another signal is given;
every pupil gives the Flag the military salute—right hand
lifted, palm downward, to a line with the forehead and close
to it. Standing thus, all repeat together, slowly: "I pledge
allegiance to my Flag and the Republic for which it
stands: one Nation indivisible, with Liberty and Justice
for all." At the words, "to my Flag," the right hand is
extended gracefully, palm upward, towards the Flag, and
remains in this gesture till the end of the affirmation:

part of an article in *The Youth's Companion* that explains how students should say the Pledge of Allegiance

1892	the Pledge of Allegiance is written and printed in *The Youth's Companion*
1923	the phrase "my flag" is changed to "the flag of the United States"
1924	the phrase "of America" is added to the pledge
1942	the Pledge of Allegiance is added to the Flag Code; Bellamy Salute is replaced with hand over heart

1943   U.S. Supreme Court rules on *West Virginia Board of Education versus Barnette*

1954   the phrase "under God" is added to the pledge

2004   the U.S. Supreme Court rules to keep "under God" in the pledge

the U.S. Supreme Court justices in 2004

Glossary

allegiance—loyal support for something or someone

citizen—a member of a particular country who has the right to live there

Columbus Day—a holiday on the second Monday of October that celebrates Christopher Columbus' arrival to North America in 1492

evidence—information and facts that help prove something or make you believe that something is true

indivisible—not able to be divided or broken into pieces

justice—fair treatment or behavior

liberty—freedom

loyal—being true to someone or something

pledge—to make a promise

primary source—an original document

religion—a set of spiritual beliefs that people follow

salute—to raise your right hand to your forehead as a sign of respect

symbol—a design or an object that stands for something else

U.S. Congress—the branch of the U.S. government that makes laws; Congress is made up of the Senate and the House of Representatives

U.S. Supreme Court—the highest and most powerful court in the United States

Read More

Fontes, Justine. *The Pledge of Allegiance*. New York: Children's Press, 2014.

Kozleski, Lisa. *The Pledge of Allegiance: Story of One Indivisible Nation*. Patriotic Symbols of America. Philadelphia: Mason Crest, 2015.

Monroe, Tyler. *The Pledge of Allegiance*. U.S. Symbols. North Mankato, Minn.: Capstone Press, 2014.

Internet Sites

FactHound offers a safe, fun way to find Internet sites related to this book. All of the sites on FactHound have been researched by our staff.

Here's all you do:

Visit *www.facthound.com*

Type in this code: 9781491482278

Check out projects, games and lots more at
www.capstonekids.com

Critical Thinking Using the Common Core

1. Reread the text about primary sources on pages 4 and 5. Give an example of a primary source you might find at home. (Integration of Knowledge and Ideas)

2. Pledging allegiance means you promise to be loyal. What does "loyal" mean? (Craft and Structure)

3. What change did President Eisenhower make to the Pledge of Allegiance in 1954? Use the text to help you with your answer. (Key Ideas and Details)

Index